# METAMORPHOSIS

## UNBECOMING AND BECOMING

## BHUMI GUPTA

to the ones who never stopped **believing** in me

# Contents

# Contents

# Foreword

**Metamorphosis** refers to the process of transformation, the changes that occur within each of us throughout our lives. But this process isn't always as simple as a caterpillar becoming a butterfly.

What about the in-between?

What about the moments when you are neither one nor the other, when you feel lost in the chrysalis, unsure of who you are as you simultaneously unbecome and become?

This is the space *Metamorphosis* explores.

It's about those times when you don't know where you're going, when all you feel is an insistent, undeniable call for change—a disruption, a revolution of the spirit. It's about the surrender that precedes the breakdown, the necessary death of the "you" you once were, to make way for the rebirth that follows a damn deep fall.

This collection is for those who are in the midst of that messy, beautiful, and often painful transformation.

# Preface

To write these poems was to lay myself bare. It was a process of confronting the parts of myself I had long tried to hide—the insecurities, the disappointments, the moments of profound vulnerability. Metamorphosis is not a comfortable read, nor was it a comfortable write.

It is an exploration of the raw, unfiltered emotions that accompany personal growth, a testament to the courage it takes to face our own "dark demons."

But it is also a story of hope.

It's about finding strength in vulnerability, about learning from our mistakes, and about embracing the messy, beautiful process of becoming. Within these pages, you'll find not just my story, but a reflection of the universal human journey toward self-acceptance and transformation. It's a reminder that even in our brokenness, there is beauty and strength, and that from the ashes of our past, we can rise stronger and more whole.

# Acknowledgements

First and foremost, I express my deepest gratitude to my father, whose unwavering belief in me has been a constant source of strength. He encouraged me to forge my own path, to resist societal pressures, and to believe in myself even when I faltered. He played an essential role in shaping the person I am today.

To my mother, thank you for your unwavering support. Your warm embraces and playful teasing have a remarkable ability to transform even the most difficult days. You have consistently filled me with hope, supported every step of my creative journey, and provided a safe space for me to share my thoughts and frustrations.

To my elder brother, thank you for your unwavering loyalty and honest guidance. Your quiet support has been invaluable, especially during challenging times. I appreciate your encouragement to be more open and to find my voice.

To my twin brother, thank you for simply being you. You have been a constant companion, guide, study partner, and friendly competitor. I am deeply grateful for your unwavering belief in my potential, a belief that has often exceeded my own.

Finally, to all those I have encountered along the way—those who have stayed and those who have moved on—thank you for the invaluable lessons you have taught me about life.

# 1. Breaking Down

Down, down, and down
In the pitch-black abyss
Round, round, and round
In a spiral with no end
Do you realize?
You're trapped in your own mind
Loud, loud, and loud
Screaming in vain
Who knows you're in pain?
Smiling and nodding
Is your pretense game
How long can you keep it up?
Until nothing remains?
Forget about others,
I'm tortured by myself
Worn out by dreams and hope,
Aimless yet passionate
But with no patience
To bear it
I go astray.
Landing off your throne
Hurts your pride
You, crumbling you

Such a tactic
To hide away
From the demons
That take over
The light and all that's good
All hope and all goals
And
No one knows
Not even you

# 2. Shattering

Like a pile of glasses,
But without any voice,
Pieces inside me are staggering,
Unable to hold tight.
The more they stay,
The deeper they pierce me.
As though all the wishes
Are strewn miles away.
You hold onto something
With so much care,
Work towards it
With so much focus,
And then sometimes
You receive despair—
a punch in the gut.
The sore taste of failure
Remains longer than
The candy of triumph,
Bruising you much deeper,
Tumbling you down like a
Snowflake.
Something melts inside you
As fear sweeps you away.

All the miracles in the shape
Of earth
Staring at you right in
The face,
Yet you're lost like
A leaf of fall,
Dried out and
Uncolored.

# 3. Crumbling

Trying to explain it through metaphors,
That building towers
Without solid foundations
And a plan,
While trying to find purpose,
Will take you far and away.
Maybe you'll get to
See stars and wonders,
Swim in the fantasy pool, but
Eventually,
The wind will rise
From the east, and
Your tower will crumble
— along with your dreams.

# 4. Hell

It didn't work out
As you thought it would,
And it hurts like hell.
You're losing your strength,
Being soaked in self-love
One minute,
Only to bask in unworthiness
The very next.
At the edge of success
And the door of insecurity,
Simultaneously.
"How to balance my coins?" you ask,
For the weight of your success
Only seems to be
Dragged down by
The fullness
Of your failures.

# 5. Helpless

Voice in my head,
Be still.
I hear you,
Every word you say,
Be still.
No need to be so loud,
Cracking open everything.
I know it's chaos,
No need to be angry,
Be still.
I hear you,
But can't do anything,
For you,
Be still.

# 6. Mourning

You sit through
The night
And stare into
The walls
Wondering
About those
"What ifs"
It stays with you
The idea of an
"Alternate ending"
The poking of
"If I had"
It haunts you
At random intervals
And when it
Gets all too consuming
You decide
At some point
Everything needs to be left
Alone
*Even your past*
*Even your pain*

# 7. Trying

There are days
When I feel
A sudden anger
Flowing in my veins,
Wanting to bleed out.
These are days when
My heart is overwhelmed
With everything around,
And how things go.
It gets tough to
Get out of that Zone.
Amidst all that,
*I forget who I am,*
Surely not someone
Who makes others
Laugh.
Sometimes
I doubt I can do that.
I forget that
For some people
I've been a listener,
Even though I'm
Bad at giving any

Advice or solutions.
I mean, If I could,
Why wouldn't I do
*That for myself?*
Be the comfort hug
To my own heart.
It's so easy to
Let doubt seep in,
Than to *try*.
Maybe recollecting
All the things
*I can do,*
*I have done,*
For me, for others.
I might get through
This crossroad.

# 8. Stumbling

Keep crying
You'll find more
Reasons to cry
Keep trying
You'll find more
Reasons to try
But how do you do so
When all you feel is numbness
*Crawling in and out*
Of you?
Some moments,
It feels like
It'll kill you,
It's so strong
You'll choke on nothing.
Other moments,
It's there, a dull ache,
Embracing you before
You even acknowledge it.
Sometimes, it's the
Residual guilt,
Cutting you,

Feeling of failure
And shame that accompany it,
Chipping you away, slowly.
Other times, it's anger,
Not directed at anyone else,
But at *yourself*,
For not doing
That *one thing*
You thought you *could* do.

# 9. Wobbling

It takes one misstep,
And you stumble,
*Wobble,*
Eventually, you *fall.*
And it also takes that
One *misstep*
For everything to crumble,
As if *coming apart,*
When actually it might not be.
You loathe yourself
For being distracted,
See yourself as a humiliation.
Waves of shame and panic
Threaten to drown you.
You set your eyes,
All your hope
On that one goal,
Putting today's happiness
On tomorrow's accomplishment.
Where are you living though?

# 10. Fear

A heart
Thrumming like
A hummingbird's
Feathers with the force
Of a hammer
*Sticky, tangled swirls*
Of indefinable colours
-some dark and frightening,
others soft and welcoming,
most fluorescent and sharp
*Barbed wires of chaos*
Choking into peaceful corners
*Shards of memories sealed*
Away in locked cages
Small little creatures humming
And working through your chest,
Resting between your rib bones,
*Trying to clean up the mess*
But,
ultimately
Making it worse
In the flurry of energy
Pure *mayhem*

# 11. Self-doubt

Up and down
It's like a roller coaster ride
To which I don't
Remember buying tickets to
*Ever,*
There's constant aching
In my soul
*Sinking deeper*
Into the black hole
Wiggling to escape
Only for curtain of
Darkness surrounding me
In its cape,
You *aren't* wearing my shoes
You *don't* know how it feels
You *can't* even see it
I am on verge of snapping,
And I do but, when
I'm alone
I don't want to be
A burden for you,
I am afraid to fall *apart*

In front of those
Who I love
With all my heart.
I know,
I've worried my heart
Far *too* much
About what I'm *worth*
That's why it shakes
When answers are
Hide to find
And invisible to see

# 12. Mockery

She does nothing
You will call 'self-harming'
Yet she's lying there
With an emptiness
Hollowing her inside
Which she doesn't know
How to fill
She doesn't want to do
Anything
Even the things of
Her preference
Don't seem interesting
Feeling guilty and empty
At the same time
She *carpeted* the floor so
*Perfectly*
No one noticed the cracked
Stone *underneath*
Yes, she succeeded
In game of pretence
And fake smiles
*So 'easily'*

They ask questions
Starting with *whys*
Mixed with curiosity
To pry
In a life that they
Only care about on *surface*
What goes deep down
Is none of their business.
Just because she carries
It *well,* doesn't mean
It isn't *weighing* her down.

# 13. Insecurity

It holds on me
*Tightly*
It creeps in
Ever so
*Slightly*
Sometimes *whispers*
Sometimes *yells*
But it will be heard
Nevertheless
I believe
I'm *strong*
But oh,
How it proves me
*Wrong!*
Self-doubt
Negativity
Hurt
To name a few,
The list goes on
It's easy for anxiety to do
Punch to the gut
Head constructs
Terrible thoughts

Stare at the mirror
And see my flaws
Disgusted and ashamed
Of my reflection
Insecurity through my eyes
And out of my mouth
Bossing me around
Tossing words without care
Watch them unravel
*I listen*
Unable to take control
It holds power
It runs deep
Permanent scars
No one can see
It presses upon my chest
I sometimes wonder,
*Am I possessed?*
But then I remember
I'm stressed
It waits
It creeps in
Ever so
*Slightly*
It holds on to me
*Tightly*

# 14. Fading

Dear heart,
Please let
These feelings fade,
And please-
Stop *filling, swelling, pushing*
At your
Confines
You're fracturing yourself
Into pieces that
Have
*Sharp, jagged edges*
They are cutting my
Fingers
Even if I try to help you
*I can't put you,*
Back together
So, stop.
Then again, at times
You're so
*Strong and quiet*
That I forget you too are
*Suffering*
*Sometimes.*

# 15. Trying Again

For a star to be born
There's one thing
That must happen
A nebula must
*collapse,*
So, *collapse*
*Crumble*
This is not your destruction,
This is your rebirth!
Resilience is born
Even when we feel
Like we are dying.
Don't hesitate!
As you accept it,
The demons
Will stop haunting
*You,*
They will be feared by
*You,* not being feared
Of *you,*
Of being unapologetically
*You!*

# 16. Burning

Sometimes what's *dead*
Must be *burned* away
To make way for new beginnings,
Sometimes you just have
To step back,
Let the brittle bits
Ignite
But…
Once the flames begin
To dance their
Destructive dance-
Don't you dare
Look the other way!
Don't you dare
Close your eyes!
Watch closely and
Let the images seer
Itself into your mind,
Remember what it looked
In the midst of
Soot,
Smoke,
Haze.

Remember
So, that you don't
Require to repeat
Same conditions
For such
Blaze
I saw my life
A vast glowing empty page
With so less written
And many more remain
So, I could do anything
Paint it any colour
Create anything
How I want
And desire

# 17. Standing

You've the ability
*To survive anything*
That's why,
Despite all the storms
Made of pain and loss,
Despite all the chaos
That you have had to endure
*You are still here*
And you're still going strong
Standing in face of gust
Let it through you
Look at yourself,
Moving with the wind
You're standing firm
There might be a war
Inside you
Yet you're here
*Fighting*
You vs You
After all its during
A storm you learn
Who you are
*Really*

So, stand up
Over your inner
Fears
Pulling at the rope
That's pushing you down
Confining you
From becoming *you*

# 18. Breathe in- Breathe out

Day by day
Moment by moment
*You'll come back*
Stronger
Every time you
Break
*You'll come back*
Softer
Wiser
Sharper
Than before
Remember this
There'll be times when
You'll feel overwhelmed
When you'll fell
As if it's over
As if this the
*End*
But
The truth is-
This is only your
*Beginning*

This is just
Another part of your
Story
Stay strong
Stay beautiful
Stay you

# 19. Building

Take as long as
You need
Take your time
*Okay?*
You are undoing yourself
Breaking apart
Collecting
Retrieving
Losing
Discovering
And at *your own pace*
This is something
We all go through
This is something
We all *need*
So *please,*

Don't be so hard on yourself
Don't let your mind
Bully your body
Don't let your heart
Cave in fear of uncertainty

You're almost there
You're almost *home*

# 20. Transforming

The place of struggle,
The act of wiggling out of a form,
To acquire a new one
Can be just another word for
*Growth,*
A sure sign that you're
*Expanding,*
Sign of real & important
*Progress.*
Changing wouldn't be
*Sweet & bright;*
It will be
Dark & murky,
Painful & pushing,
Unraveling the truths
You've carried in your body,
Facing your own
Created demons,
Complete uprooting
Before *becoming.*
It might bring you
To your knees,

But it will be
*Worth it.*

# 21. Blooming

*Remember* how it feels
To be proud to be you,
To look in the mirror
And be in awe of you;
*Remember* what it was like
Before
You told yourself-
You aren't good enough,
Buried parts of yourself
Alive,
Piling doubt and loathing
Onto your body like
Soil.
Now, only you can
Bring *you* back
*To life.*
Let it bloom,
Change,
Shed,
Turn,
Fall away,
Fall apart,
Come undone,

Be uncovered,
Unform - reform
*Let it be*
Open your eyes
To life, as it is
Right now.
Look within your heart
Then ask yourself
What you truly deserve
And you'll realize
Even the saddest part
Of you
Wants to
*Bloom with grace*

# About The Author

Bhumi's writing journey began as a personal quest for self-understanding, a way to navigate the turbulent emotions of adolescence. Choosing writing as a form of self-expression, she found a powerful outlet for her thoughts and feelings. Now, writing is an essential part of her life, informing her perspective and shaping her understanding of the world. Her work delves into universal themes of societal observations, common beliefs, and the profound impact of emotions. Bhumi believes that love extends far beyond romantic contexts; it is a boundless and pervasive force that permeates all aspects of existence.

# Connect With Author

Sharing these poems was a deeply personal experience, and I'm grateful you've taken the time to read them. I invite you to connect and share your own journey.

You can find me on Instagram **@theevocativeme** or reach me via email at **theevocativeme@gmail.com**.

I value your thoughts and insights.